dream

books

Chalisha

© Copyright Sheri Hauser 2016
© Copyright for art by Karna Peck, KPO
Published by Glorybound Publishing
SAN 256-4564
10 9 8 7 6 5 4 3 2 1
Printed in the United States of America
ISBN 978-1-60789-295-3 1-60789-295-2
Library of Congress Cataloging-in-Publication data is
available on file.
Hauser, Sheri, 1957-
        Chalisha/Sheri Hauser
        Includes biographical reference.
1. Christian Writing.   2. Inner conflict
I. Title

www.gloryboundpublishing.com

The painting used for the cover of *Chalisha* is
from the gallery of Karna Peck. More of her art
may be seen on her website *www.karnapeck.com.*

DREAM CACHË

Welcome to Sheri's dream cache releasing what has been kept hidden until now. There are
stores of riches kept in a vault up to this day, which open the door of understanding the
voice of God in dreams as answers to prayer. The wind, the storm, the rain and the
lightening of God is coming. Feel the wind? There is always a gentle breeze just
before the tornado. Oh how we have looked for the eye of the storm in this
world in which we live, yet we have not found it. We have prayed, yet we
are not healed. We have spent countless hours on our knees without
finding our deliverance. Our children remain on drugs; our families
are still in bondage; we are yet poor and destitute. Our Churches are
poor, filled with empty pews and singers off cue. Where are the answers
to our prayers? We have been tricked by our enemies. They have snuck in and
left seeds of doubt which grew into a cancer eating away at our faith in God. Our vision
has been clouded by our own
sinfulness and lust for the things of this world. Yet we continue to seek for a force outside
©ourselves which will save us from this dreadful condition which we are in. Where is He?
Take encouragement, friends, I have brought a fresh shipment of hope: It's the hope of
hearing the voice of God for yourself. Just like Moses heard the voice of the Lord and
brought Salvation to the Children of Israel, He is bringing the same today. Has God
changed? No. Suppose you ask a question in prayer: Do you expect an answer?
There is one, you know? I am here to help you reach out to God in a special way
and enable the enemies of doubt within your life to be crushed and conquered.
What I bring is a bridge to faith. We attempt to reach a God we do not
know; only have heard about from those going on before us. But, when
we reach into that darkness, we are unsure of a connection: Will there
be a hand reaching back to us? We don't really know. That is faith,
my friend. Faith reaches into the unknown seeking something you
are unsure of while trusting that there will be an answer on the
other side. Welcome to my dream Cachë. It is like a jewelry
box filled with gems, sparkling in the moonlight: dreams
that come to life as the voice of God dances through my
head night after night. And, He wants the same for
you. He told me, so. Your dreams and visions
can be a bridge to a relationship with God
giving encouragement, hope, help, and
direction hidden in this vault of
wondrous pictures
sent straight
from
heaven.
I have propped open
for you five doors
and a window .
I encourage
you to
learn to seek God through learning to understand His voice as it
comes to you His way, now as you are comfortable accepting it. Remember,
God came in thunder, storm and a wind in times before. Why wouldn't He now? May
I present this shipment of Grace. For it is by the Grace of God that we are saved. Remember that.

TABLE OF CONTENTS

Chalisha

My two me's: A book on the battle within

By
Sheri Hauser

Glorybound Publishing
Camp Verde, Arizona
October 2016

LETTER FROM THE AUTHOR

There is a conflict going on within each of us. It is a battleground of who we are VS who we want to be; who I show you and who I show myself. Sometimes it seems like I am schizophrenic having a variety of faces. This book is on the inner battle of the entire mess. Do not confuse this book with demonic possession (read katísha or Sinactía for that aspect). What this book is about Paul writes in the Bible; I do what I don't want to do... wretched man that I am. Surely, there is grace of God enough to cover this type of doing and undoing.

However, we are met with a variety of expectations from individuals and God as well as ourselves. Each day; we need to sort these all out to try to become who we are intended to be, molded into the purposes of God's intention.

Chalisha is a thought provoking book written from dreams (with interpretation) as well as inspirational writings all on the subject of the inner conflict. Initially, I wanted to entitle the book 'My Haunted House' because sometimes it seems like someone from my past is living within my soul. These may be the echo of the words of my parents as I grew up or the refrain of my personal expectations kicking around in my brain.

The challenge is to sort through all of these expectations and come out with some realistic answer. In the Bible it says 'Be ye holy as I am holy'. This seems like a high standard for someone living in the flesh, however, it is the word of God and not up for argument. So, how do we mesh all of this thinking together to come out with an answer we can live with?

I think the grace of God extends much further than we can ever imagine and if we are willing to be brutally honest with Him, He will come into our haunted house and help us kick out those vagrant thoughts which keep kicking the walls of our mind. Welcome to my version of Chalisha.

My 2 Mes

My me to me and my me to you.
For my me to me isn't my me to you.
You know it's true.
How can it be? How can I be free?
Cuz, me to me may not agree.
For, I didn't even agree with me.
Am I two or three?
I am not sure. How can this be?
If I'm not sure who I am, then how can I tell it to you?
My me to thee isn't free to be told to me and thee.
Bound up in a ball wound tighter, that's all.
My me is mine and it may not be time.
But, it's all I got. It's my lot.
My me is me and it may not be free.
But, it's all I got and I fought the fight
and, I fret the yet, and lost the bet.
My me is mine, over the line.
When I ask the man, He tells the plan
and, I see the one,
the free we me and I know who I am.
He develops the plan
Now, meet the we me
And, you will see us three.

Peep hole of faith

We reached the end of our mortal understanding, face of guilt, with blood soaked hands; we realized we had nothing with which to barter. Either, we face God now or wait until later. So, we took our chances and we reached through the key hole of the door and entered into the secret place of the most high God. It was there that we found the bed He had laid the broken body of His Son, on.

And, once again we came face to face with the reality of the reason Jesus was sent to earth; to be broken and die for our sins. And, the Father keeps this body in His room, now. But, any time we want, we can visit this room.

The door is closed because the spiritual world is separate from the physical world. But, friend, He has placed within our heart a key that opens the door. It is a key to understanding the things of God. And, when we peak through the gateway of faith, we cross over; we look through the peep hole into the Father's bedroom and by trust in His provision, we are able to cross over from the place where we are to a place we need to be. We pass from sinful to holy; mortal to immortal; death to life. We become alive.

But, it is in this place that we see the blood continues to drip off His fingers one drop at a time falling on the fine oriental carpet. And, this blood doesn't clot because it is alive ever flowing from the heart that continues to beat.

For, the body of Jesus lives through us when we pass through by faith and grasp the true meaning of the sacrifice of Jesus. It's the peep hole of faith.

Chapter 1

INTIMACY
Who I think I am

Split Personality

The Dream: *The woman neglected her dog, so he died. When she learned of it, she was overwhelmed with guilt and it split her personality. She was actually split. Satan was mocking her despair. And, being unwilling to allow him a show, I ran after her to gather her back together. She had no control. Despair had taken over. And, I made her husband and someone else admit that there were spiritual problems before I moved to repair the damage. Because I knew certainly, God could fix this mess.*

Interpretation: The woman neglected that which had been entrusted to her care. Like being given a talent and neglecting it; when she refused to feed it, then it died. When we refuse to care for that which as been entrusted to us, it dies. Like not watering a plant, it will soon fade away and wilt in the sun.

But, within the dream, when the dog dies, the woman is overwhelmed with guilt and it comes to her causing her personality to become split. When we neglect the gifts God has entrusted to us and they die, sometimes we may feel guilt and remorse. The message of the dream is that this guilt is from Satan sent to damage the individual's personality.

When we refuse to care for that which has been entrusted to us and it dies, when we feel guilt, what should our response be? Guilt feelings are sent by the Holy Spirit with the purpose of demonstrating victory over Satan. Because when we claim forgiveness through the blood of Jesus, immediately, Satan is defeated all over again just like at the Cross of Jesus. What happens is that when we sin, it sets up a spiritual battlefield. The sin of neglect led to death of that which was meant to live. When the death became evidence of the sin, the woman was overcome with guilt. It was the spirit of guilt 'as an entity' which split her personality. She became at war within. The sin caused her spirit to wage war against herself. This allowed her heart to become a play field of Satan and he made a mockery of her sinfulness with a display by tearing her personality apart.

Did she cause it? Of course. Because when she refused to do that which had been given to her to do which was to care for her pet, then the spirit was permitted to take control over her. She became at war within. The spirit of neglect was set against the spirit of responsibility; the spirit of despair was set against the spirit of joy. And as the joy was taken, it was as if that piece was sliced off her personality. When Satan mocked her lack of responsibility with the 'truth' then the spirit of responsibility floated off...

At that point she became separated from who she really is supposed to be: a forgiven person with victory over the Devil.

So, in the dream, I confront the spiritual issues of 'split personality' and show them that when she deals with the sin, she will have victory over the issues which split her within.

...I will send the Counselor...when he comes, he will convict the world of guilt in regard to sin and righteousness and judgment: in regard to sin, because men do not believe in me; in regard to righteousness, because I am going to the Father, where you can see me no longer; and in regard to judgment because the prince of this world now stands condemned. John 16.7-10

Heart Cry

I told you to pray
But, I didn't know how
I asked you to ask
Is there more than a bow?

I wanted you to seek
But, where are you Lord?
I gave you a sign
It was more than I could afford.

I screamed in your face
How was I to know?
I offered free grace
I thought it was merely a show.

But, I needed some help
Did you think I wouldn't come?
And, the help never came.
You used it and then some.

I gave all I could
Where was my help
I met the need
Abandoned I felt.

Like two roads that passed
We each went our own way
I went mine
Never heard what you had to say

But I yelled out the window

As my car passed on by
Waiting for you to follow
Hearing my cry.

But, I couldn't hear you, Lord
Though my need was intense
The radio blaring loud
With noise that was immense
Phones ringing in my ear
And many people near
I didn't hear the call
That was all.

We call to God but miss His response because, God answers with His Spirit. So, when we call with our voice and He answers with His heart, we don't hear it because we are not listening on that level. Heart tones are different from audible tones.

Our heart can cry out to God and He will respond bringing comfort and peace.

Pulling Someone's String

The Dream: *We are all in the car with mother and someone hands me a talking doll. I pull the string and she talks. When I pull the string, she tells me that there is a guy by the name of ... that hates me. I can't seem to catch the name, and I keep trying to get it, but am unable to understand what she is saying clearly. I want to prepare myself for who hates me, but can't if I don't get what she is saying, so I ask my step-father if he has a recorder. He manages to locate an old tape recorder, but doesn't have any tapes to go into it.*

My mother sleeps with a pink pig. I think it's weird, but she thinks it is adorable.

I go to a city on a hill and try to drive a truck in a tight spot. I need to make a delivery. Someone comes to try to harm me, but God assures me that He will protect me no matter where I am at or what name they go by. Know your protector. He is a mystery of many mysteries. I bring this truck in and park it at this high mountain restaurant. He is the one seeking to harm me, not me to harm him.

Interpretation: It has been put into our hand to pull the string of the one who chants hate against us. We don't have to bother to learn his name, because we already know his name. It is the enemy behind every one that breaths threats against a child of God. The one we need to know is the Father of Mysteries and He will reveal all mysteries to us that we need to know to protect us. We should not focus on learning the enemy, but the one who protects us. The message of the dream is that our Father does not keep records of those who breathe threats, so we should not either. We should not hold grudges against those who have been mean to us. Let Him keep them in account for the wrong doings that they have done against you.

Mother wisdom pigs the night. She is the one who guards dreams: listen to her.

The message that God has put into my hand to deliver is like driving a semi into a tight spot, but He will help me to deliver. It is food for the hungry that will serve many. Food for prayer.

In between who I am
help me to return to the place I am supposed to be.

Water in the basement

Some choose to believe a lie because they refuse to deal with the truth.

Because the problem with believing the truth is that it overruns other areas and you loose all control. Like water getting into the basement, there might be other stacks of old magazines which could get wet. There are things that we are not willing to deal with, which will come to surface, forcing us to respond.

And, we put on a face of 'pity me' when the truth is that we are controlling the environment to keep ourselves comfortable. We have taken all the bad stuff in our lives and tossed it into a room in the basement and shut the door.

But, when someone who walks in truth comes along, he opens the basement doors of your life. And, if the Holy Spirit wasn't involved, we might be able to push him away and slam the door in his face, but when the Holy Spirit brings enlightenment, then He comes in through his life like water and begins to fill the basement where we have continued to stash stuff which we should have tossed out long ago.

So, the only thing we can do is declare a burglary has happened. 'My space has been invaded." We say, "He came into a place where I didn't invite him."

And, we act indignant.

But, the problem is that it is the Holy Spirit which has invaded that basement, not the other person. People don't indwell others; only God can indwell.

So, no wonder there is such a reaction; the individual feels that you have caused their house to spring a leak which is irreparable because there is no way that person can fix the problem; you can't control the Holy Spirit. He comes wherever He wants.

I say, just stand back; because when the spring begins to flow into a basement, eventually it will reach the upper floors pushing the individual into action. The Holy Spirit is faithful to convict the world concerning sin, judgment and righteousness. He tells the truth and encourages its flow through out life.

God's Shadow

Soon the sun will rise with a mighty power never seen
Before; the powerful hand of the almighty God.
To press through and part people, soul
and spirit. They will know it's Me.
The shadow will
overwhelm.
I am walking toward
you, from the end forward.
Like a shadow moves
in front of a
person,
My
shadow
is moving
in
front of
My presence
that will meet you
face to face at the end of the world.

Two Souls

The overflow of my soul fills my other.
My other needs that I don't know I have yet.
Do I have two souls?
Sort of.
It's like the one you are aware of
and the one you aren't.
For, you don't even know your own soul,
you know?
When you become slightly depressed,
at which point do you realize it?
There is a position between when we are and we don't
realize it.
It is that space that God's grace fills
with the overflow.
The left over prayers, like clumps of bread left
over from the feeding of the five thousand, they feed later
on.
They become the late night snack for those who are
hungry after while.
We have an 'after while' with our soul, as well.

There are times we actively feed it,
and there are the rest times.
It is in those times of rest that we see truly where we stand
with God.
For, who talks then?
Do we hear television programs, or sports?
Do we hear our family's voices?
Does our job invade our mind
during this quiet time?

If our soul is filled with God's words,
then He will be anxious to catch up on the
latest.
He will have a lot to say.
Our soul will overflow with His words.
Or our souls will overflow with words to Him.
For, sometimes, I can't keep quiet.
I burst with love toward Him.
I want to tell Him how grateful I am
for all He has done for me.
I can't wait to tell Him.
Especially, if a lot has happened.
The goal, I guess, is to get these two souls to
merge.

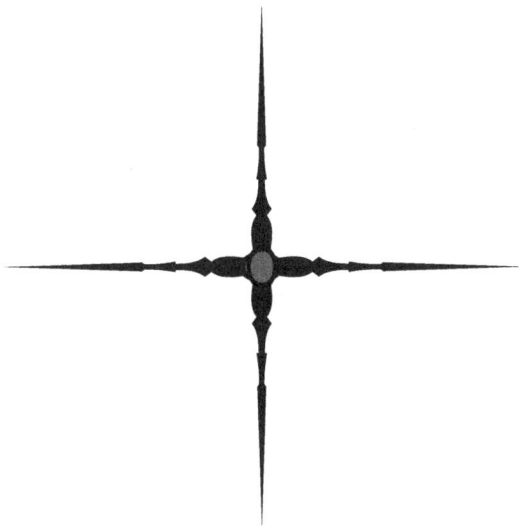

Chapter 2

SELF
Who I want to be

Ever Sure

I had a hope of my own, yet it depended upon you
There was a way I needed you to go, to push on through
I had a dream; a vision in my head
A desire to fulfill. You saw yours instead
I had a hope of my own, yet it hinged upon your door
A wake of opportunity marked across the floor
evidence upon evidence compiled alone
Fulfillment of desire, now turned into stone
I had a hope of my own, one given to me
yet I see, now, the problem that I didn't see
hinged upon the hinge, hung the door for both of us
each on our own side, fearing what we must
You had a hope of your own, and one you gave to me
But it didn't match my outfit, so I set it free
The hope that we had, we never had together
yet, a hope if it could, would last forever
Hinged upon a promise, a hope will endure
ever sure.

The Island of Runaground

Battered by the storms of life, she sought refuge under a log that had drifted ashore. The boat had gone down under the intense pounding of the waves against the hull of her hard head. She was going to do it 'her way'. And, so it was. She did. Without listening to others, she sculpted her future, her figure and her career. Beautiful, yet not adored; Adorned, yet untrue, set on a mission of success built from mental strain and determination, she pushed the mentally fragile ones aside, refusing to allow their intrusion into her thoughts.

With steel eyes and a hardened heart, she pushed aside emotion laughing at reproach. She was right; her life proved it was so. Setting sail alone; this fair weather queen adorned her own bow for there was no need for another. Everyone knows that a craft has but one bow needing to be adorned. She did it herself. She sailed up and down the coast keeping close in to shore to be sure to be noticed her time was all taken.

"Surely," she reasoned, "A tight schedule proves ones worth; therefore, I am valuable."

So, she sailed. Back and forth year after year up and down the coastal waters rightly adorning her craft with herself.

At first there were onlookers, gazing from ashore. Novelty demands attention. But, soon they were called to their own purpose and turned from hers. Ah, she stacked up fleeting moments one upon another; pressed into short relationships without depth. Together they almost mounted to something; yet in the rain of time they melted.

Without an audience, who would dance? Without onlookers, why adorn yourself? If no one cares, why take the boat out at all?

So she tied it to the dock in the fall and paid a mooring fee. For, who knows, perhaps she will be sailing again next season? There is a cost to being tied to a stable relationship. And, for a while, she paid it.

But, when spring came and the flowers began to bloom, there was hope in the air. She went to the dock and visited her vessel. She buffed and waxed; contemplated and mulled ideas; to stay tied for another year or launch out once more.

Surely there was some new audience that needed to recognize the beauty of her stature. Amidst fair weather, she set a course due East; fixing her gaze upon the horizon she sailed into unknown waters.

Without a compass, she followed her reason. Without compassion for those she left behind, sailing away was easy. A hard heart can know no other because in order for a heart to connect to someone else it must be softened to have the strands intertwined with the other one. Hers was as a stone; she was used to tossing it into the boat whenever she desired; and sailing off into the wind of her whim.

She ran aground at midnight at 'who knows where'. How could she know? There was no compass and the lights had gone out long ago.

Recognizing she was in a perilous position having the boat torn from asunder, she prepared to drown. Saying her prayers, and taking a final gasp of the night air, she jumped overboard. Her body prepared for the worst, she was surprised that the water was not cold, but warm.

With plenty of air in her lungs it was a natural inclination to push off the bottom when her toes reached it with their extension. And, the push was just enough to bring her to the surface.

Aha, what do you know? The shore was right there. Why would she opt to drown when she could swim ashore? Pride, remorse and refusal to face what she had turned her back on? Were they reasons enough to die?

It was her choice; and, who would know? She could make it seem as though it was not her fault; being a victim of circumstances. After all, she was aground on a rock. The caption could read, "She went down between a rock and a hard place".

Yet, she went ashore and hid from herself on an island in the middle of nowhere alone amidst the storm and buried her face in remorse hating herself for being who she was. The devil taunted her in the un-met dreams of her desire until the sun came up.

Hearing a noise, she squinted her eyes to see a vision appearing in some distance and growing ever near. As much as she tried to hide her eyes; who can hide from a vision?

The man with deep wrinkles in his face came right up to her and held out his hand. Without a word, she took it. He had no request from her. She could be anyone she wanted with him. So, she left her past behind and went fishing. Sure, the wreckage was in the distance, but neither of them mentioned it.

And, the wreckage has become a breeding ground for new fish. So, the old man and the lost sailor dine and share with others on the Island of Runaground around the fires of delight in a place where the only expectation that they have from one another is being who they really are.

Alone amidst

Alone amidst adrift in a sea of faces
none known, yet every one known by Him
Alone amidst adrift in a life of races
none known by me, yet all intimately known within
Alone amidst sailing on the fair blue seas
one man among many pushed by the breeze
Alone, yet not alone by much; a touch
will see; set you free to be
Not alone anymore; you have found the shore
come dance with us, and dance some more
Alone, amidst the morning kiss
heavenly dew to you. No more blue
To find the find, intertwined
set the rope, the hope, release, don't grope
Launch your boat, cross the moat
Open the door, from across the floor
alone amidst, send a kiss
for one you love, God above
let it fly and He will send
the kiss from above, a cheek to tend
to mend, alone amidst a broken heart.

Me and My Dad

What happened to me and my dad? We used to love without reserve.
What happened to me and my dad? How did it all go bad?
What have I done, the pain I have dealt? How did
this happen when I never felt? My emotions
were dead and my flesh was all dried My
spirit was weak and I believed the lie.
What happened to me and my dad?
The love we had went south one day
and, the relationship we knew went astray.
How I loved him since I was a lad, certainly it makes us
both sad. We have stumbled, staggered and strewn our lives
into a wretched pile. What happened to me and my dad?
Certainly, he understands how sad I am, just as he is
for me. For, certainly, he knows my heart, my
yearning desire to be free. The bondage
I bare is simply too great, I bow
and continue to endure
the berate.
But,
surely,
he
knows,
doesn't
he, I ask?
That I dearly miss
what we had in the past.
For, what happened to me and my dad? Where did he go?
I tried to look for him, he certainly must know.
Somehow, he thought it was all a show.
But, my heart bares the truth as it has always done.
I never meant to go astray, and be dependent on only this one.
For, no one but me knows the despair, the pain and disrepair of my soul.
How I long for his arms, his warmth and his love to make me whole.

But, what happened to me and my dad? Where did we go bad?
Try as I may, I will cannot rest this day So, to You, My Father,
I lift my heart and pray. Bring the answer, drop it into my spirit today.
I give you my life, set me on Your bay. I need repair, I need to be
fixed and made new. Oh, Holy Father, come restore me to You.
Where did we go wrong? What have I done? Certainly, I
have tried to live in a world of only one. Forgive my
selfish heart, renew a new mind in my head. Grant
me some grace to live for others instead. Forgive
my chasing after kites, help me to chase Your might.
For, my might never turned out, and Yours is for sure.
And, by Your light I will see the way
Please direct me, dear Lord, to Your way, I pray.
Now I see what happened to me and my dad
How I left him when I was just a lad.
And I see, now, dear Father above,
how he has helped me come
back. And I thank you
both that by a
miracle
at Your
hand,
he has
filled my lack.
Praise You, dear Lord, I lift my heart to
your place. Give me new life, may I enter into
Your grace. Fresh faith each day and protection from
Sin. Grant me Your provision within. Because I know
what happened between me and my dad And I thank
You. How You have made my heart glad.
Praise Your holy name, I lift
my voice on high
Bless me
please,
bring me nigh.
Be my Lord, my Savior, my Father divine
For, now I know, what
is mine. Two father I have, not
merely one alone. I have been given another,
it has been shown. What happened didn't just happen
here on earth, but in a greater dimension before I was given birth.

Dock House

The dream:

God has put us in a precarious place. It is like a house at the end of a long dock. The wind is blowing and the waves are striking the pillars of the dock house. As the rain from the storm blows sideways it seems impossible to make it through alive. At the very least the dock will be torn apart from the shore and we will barely survive. Then, two hornets are able to enter into the house from the side door. I realize that the best way to get rid of them is to open the other doors and let the wind blow them out, but the rain is pouring and the wind is gusting hard. I go to the far right corner of the building and open the door. I see a porch area which I never noticed before and consider this as an option.

But, as I look down at the waves, I loose perception and it seems as though the dock begins to move and will be torn from the shore. My eyes follow the pillars along the dock to the shore and I can clearly see that the dock is firmly anchored to the bedrock and is not moving. My perception was altered when I focused on the rage of the storm rather than the purpose. So, I move to the left side of the structure along the front and open the door. There is a covering there which I never noticed before and it is very protected. Certainly, I can open this door and permit the breeze to gently blow through and take away these hornets.

Interpretation:

This vision is firmly embedded with very strong pillars into the bedrock of where it is supposed to be. It is an extension out over the sea. It is put there to help others to see God's grace and love; Mercy and forgiveness amidst all circumstances. He has put me there with those whom He trusts (you to be one). But, in the dream a couple of hornets have entered in by the side door. Indeed, the enemy sends messengers who will torment us if we allow it to be so. These messengers will cause us to run and hide from the original purposes which God intends for us to do. The messengers of harm are indicated within the dream: Uncertainty of the stability of the vision and calling of God, and focusing on the wrong things. In the dream, when I opened the wrong door, I began to focus on the raging storm and water....and all of a sudden I became disoriented to the point that I suspected that the entire dock was moving away from the shore.

When we focus on the storm or the hornets which have entered into our secure place, we become fearful and want to run and hide. It is the sure intention of the enemy to want us to run from the calling and purposes of God. Our faith wavers; never the ability of God to sustain us. The place where He has provided is sure as it is embedded deep within the bedrock of His calling and purposes. I guess it is OK to check to make sure that the dock is still attached to the shore every once in a while.

The hope in the dream is that when I open the other door, I find a porch that I never knew was there which provides a place of covering and security allowing the breeze to blow through getting rid of the hornets.

I think this dream talks....I think that sometimes we begin to run from the things which would cause us pain and we look for a way out of it. But, we need to be careful which doors we open because some of them will cause us to become unstable. Remember, the porch is our covering and we can find security there.

Excuses

As it is, I long to go to sleep so You can talk to me.
I am sorry Lord.

Because, I am so noisy during the day that I can't hear
Your voice whispering into my soul. I'm sure I could find
some excuses for not paying clear attention to You, but
none of them are any good.

Daily New You

And, what would happen if you dedicated your heart to
Jesus every day of your life?

If, you asked Him to cleanse you of your sins and make
you new every single day?

What would happen, then?

Does He make you new each time? How many new
yous does He have in that heavenly closet of His? I think
He has as many as you are willing to use. And, each time
we trade in our old self, and ask for a new you, He grants
our request with an increased purity. Less of the things
that hold you back and more of the things that allow you
to take flight.

And, my goal is that I will be light enough to easily
have my feet lift from the ground when Jesus comes back
to take me with Him.

Stranded on the Rooftop

I stand on the rooftop and call out to you.
Is there anyone out there?
I scream with all my breath, to hear only my echo return.
Is there anyone out there?
My home has been destroyed, my life a scorn
I am left all alone, simply to die and morn.
Where is did my help go, I wish I knew?
How can I survive without life anew?
For, my life is at risk and my family all apart.
There seems no one to listen to my crying heart.
Is there any one out there?
From the flood of my thoughts, my possessions are afloat.
I sit here on the roof looking at all the writ I wrote.
For all is lost and nothing is to be had
If my life is all alone. Certainly that would be bad.
Is there anyone out there?
For, day after day, year after year I call out to you
A God who happens to be your Father all the way through
And you thought I wasn't listening, how do you think I feel?
For, I have been stranded aloft, left to fish without a reel.
I have called out day and night, running through your mind
And again and again, I have been someone you could not find.
Is there anyone out there?
How my voice burns for a response to my plea
To hear from my family would make my heart glad with glee.
Yet, I paint signs in the sky and dip my brush to color the clouds.
I write day and night, yet your mind remains in shrouds.
Come to My house, and rescue my lonely heart.
Be my deliverer, bring your part.
For, this heart is separated by the gap you refuse to cross.
It's a line in the sand that has become dental floss.
Stuck in your teeth, becoming a grind,
This gap of sin only I can unwind.

Filling the chocolates

The dream:

I get drilled, filled, whitened to blue. Me and the fillers become very good friends.

Plus, I have a problem with my sugar levels. I need more. And my friend is so surprised that I am like her.

There is a lot of daily drilling, cleaning, whitening and all. There is a sweetness overwhelming the body.

Rich and poor will all get in line to be filled and sweetened because they all need it inside. There is no difference between us. Their social status doesn't correlate with the spiritual status.

There was a young girl brought by her mother in fancy garments. I knew they were expensive because I had seen them on the cover of a magazine. She laid them all aside to stand in line for the sweetness of God. Corianta. Beneath those rich garments she was still just a girl in need like us all.

Interpretation:

And as a young woman, wisdom has brought me to the place where I have laid aside my fancy garments to stand in line for the sweetness of God because I realize that there is no difference between being rich and poor. The only thing that makes us poor is not receiving what God has for us. When we realize we are poor then we will seek His riches. Then, and only then will I be truly rich.

Gateway to Immortality

Jesus walked the gateway to immortality. By His service to us we can be cleansed and filled to serve others. It was His service to us that occurred when He went to His field of ministry which opened the door enabling us to be able to go to others. He led the tour but showing the way. His life was a display of how one is trained in the things of God learning the Scriptures and holiness in living and growing in humility waiting until He was released to do what God had called Him to do.

And, the Devil could not lay a finger on Him because He walked into the holiness of God with clear direction and agility. Only His frailty within the flesh stopped Him. And, that is the same thing that stalls now.

Echo of My life

Echo's my life: my own dreams crashed and I clung by faith to the top rail of another house. It was a touch with danger and a dance with death because eyes were not open. I warn them: crush the grape to get the juice. Not until I was broken apart could it all flow. Multiple of gifts and books. It's a dip and soar like an eagle. Swoop in low. Skud runner behind enemy lines. Run the line with death.

Mothering Dream

The Dream:

She didn't mean to, but she killed her mother duck. Now, the baby duck is standing over his dead mother. Her neck has been broken and there is no hope of recovery. So I say, "Bring the baby to another mother; to one who knows how to raise ducks. She may tend to it and try."

Interpretation:

His hope had died and his vision completely shattered. He stood over the broken dream like standing over the body of his mother who died a traumatic death. But, by long term relationship, I enabled them to be brought to another place. And, if they are able to become acceptable with their new mother, she will raise them up. Their hope is revived and raised up anew.

Ducks are different from other birds in that they mate for life and tend to one another. I used to tell one of my daughters that she had friends like a duck…in that she had life-time friends rather than spur of the moment friends who she released to find others. I think that certain individuals have more of a 'duck' personality in that when they make friends, they expect to keep them for life. I'm a duck.

In the dream the baby duck ends up without a mother and I suggest that he be taken to another mother to be raised. I admit that the other mother may not agree to care for him, but it is his best option under the circumstances, because at this point he is without a duck mother. He really needs someone who understands him as a duck.

I think that the duck is an allegory related to what God has given you as a life-time dream. He has embedded within your heart that which would ultimately please you and bring honor to Him. But, sometimes we kill that 'mother' of all dreams. By our own hand, we bring about the demise of that which would raise us up to be that which is the most we could be. There is another clue in the dream given to me. It is the word 'hope'. We allow our hope to become foul (fowl). *Nice play on words*. The dream is clear that the demise occurs at our own hand. We kill it.

It seems to me that there are a lot of dreams that die in between their origination and the goal. Again, part of the answer is given by the use of ducks. We need to grab onto those dreams and accept them as a life-long friend. The message says that the dream (momma duck) raises the duckling. What that means is that the dream does not raise itself, but gives birth to a son. A dream is a vision of what is to happen. It didn't happen yet, or it wouldn't be a dream. Like a baby in the womb, the dream needs to be birthed and then raised up to become its intention. A dream is like a template or a floor plan that gives a model for building. It is not the building. The correlation is that the duckling is the building. The dream (mother duck) gives birth to that which will be raised up to look exactly like her. So, if the duckling follows his mother (and ducklings do follow their mother) he will become very similar to her. So, if you follow the design of the dream that God has given into your heart as a vision for your ministry, when it is fully grown (reached maturity over time) then it will look very similar to the dream.

Yet the dream says that many have killed their mother without intention. The dream was birthed by the vision. To rise up a dream it takes desire, determination and discipline. We must have a long term relationship to enable the dream to be raised up to become its intended purpose.

The part of the dream where I say that perhaps another will raise up the duckling is a profound teaching. What it means is that if you have killed your mother inadvertently....or by loss of hope the vision of your ministry has died, then you may ask for another one. Yet, the dream is tentative in that I will request that the other mother assume care of the duckling, but it is not automatic, but according to her desire. You see, the problem is that if God gave you a dream that would take some 30 years to mature, and you burned up some 27 years of it already, then it is not automatic that you will be given another and expect to be raised up under the wing of another. But, you can ask.

Lesson on intimacy

He called us all together for a lesson and everyone was surprised at what he had to say. That the ability to be intimate with Him is from our side, not His. How we had waited for Him to provide some things He left with us long ago through the Father, Son, and Holy Spirit. But, we come to Him and forget to bring it. We leave it at home.

Transparency

He bought my ability to be transparent with Him.
I thought He would keep it at His house,
but He didn't.
He sent it home with me.
I own my own ability to be transparent.

The difference between the voice and the person

There is a difference between the voice of someone and him. The voice is the sound that is made to form words when we put air behind it. That is exactly why some can't hear the voice of God. They have no air.

Didn't Jesus say, "I breathe on you and you will receive the Holy Spirit?"

In order for someone to breathe on you, you need to be close enough to feel it, but, we are too afraid to get that close.

Chapter 3

EXPECTATIONS
Who I should be

In the middle

*In the middle of a bad generation, I will still continue to
reach out to those for whom I have given my life blood for.
I have nothing to loose, and a few more souls to gain.
The reverent heart of God listens to your prayers.
Pardon me if I talk to you about your soul.
Satan would like to keep you busy until you breath your
final breath. But, that is not my plan.
I have some rest built into the program.
Because, if you turn over your soul to my care,
I will fight those battles you now, have no control over.
I will enable rest through victory in the Spirit world of
which you have no control. Don't fool yourself.
And don't let Satan trick you.
Either he is in charge, or I am. There is no three way
battle. You think you have a kingdom? What do you
control? The control you cherish is your own will.
Do you think you can go down the middle between God
and Satan minding your own business?
If you are not in either kingdom, you are left as a cast out.
The power of God comes to meet us, we pray, he rescues,
then we become backed up again. But the forward
movement is staggering, enabling wonderful power.*

A Disability in our Walk

A serious disability exists. Satan told them their legs are broken and they believe it. The disability lies in the area of willingness to step out on faith.

Satan has told them that they can't walk because I won't support them. He has undermined faith in provision which stunts growth within ministry.

So, they won't walk because they think their legs are broken. It is me that empowers my body to walk.

Just like yours. Your mind wills, your legs to move, then I empower them. So, with the body of Christ, my mind wills the legs of my body to walk toward my purposes, then I empower them.

The hoax of Satan is to have you wait for the provision before you walk. It is not true with your own body, why would it be different with the Church?

One of the problems is insecurity in the direction of the movements for the walk. People aren't sure what they are supposed to do. They have inability to interpret the messages that I give. There is an interruption between my mind and the feet. Like a synaptic gap, the messages aren't getting from my brain to my feet. Part of the insecurity is that they only have one channel. They think I only speak through the Scriptures. The Scriptures are the word. I speak through my word. I give my word daily to all who are hungry.

They have omitted the part that I can speak into their spirit. Through that channel, they can open up seven other channels. Think. With 8 channels all telling an account of the whether for the next week, would you be more sure?

My presence will tell you it's me. My wisdom will tell you why. My knowledge will give insight as to the connection between other aspects of my character and plan. The spirit of counsel will help with the collaboration between scripture and my words for today.

All through I will continue to draw you closer with the fear of the Lord. With the Spirit of understanding, you will get the whole idea of the Kingdom of God on earth. And, with the Spirit of might, my will is empowered. We walk hand in hand, then you can walk on stilts. Amen.

Hard Nose

Those whom I came to do not recognize me because they have been tricked to believe in a God that does not exist. He is a hard nosed character; A stiff father, quick to discipline his children.

This God is intent on standing by the chalk board and writing chalk marks for good behavior and reading the Bible. But, how they sadden my heart.

For, they spend more time reading what I wrote than talking to me. And, I am standing right here.

Restoration of things Abandoned

The Dream:
And, I saw that, once again they are building in the
places once abandoned. It's as if the spider webs are
being used in a good way because they had become so
thick around these houses of abandonment that they
enabled the snow to pile on the roof protecting each
structure. And, now they are returning to that place of
abandonment and they are building grand structures in
this country by the freeway next to where the train passes
daily.

Interpretation:

It was the spirit of abandonment that was so thick over
you that it covered your ears and eyes so you could not see
your true purpose. But, indeed, I have not abandoned you.
But, you, my love, have learned the truth that Satan is evil
and I am good. Even what he tears up you have learned,
I can use for My benefit. It was your life, as you went
through all the pain that I have used: Your willingness to
allow Me to heal the spirit of abandonment and fill it with
My love has provided the covering to protect the building
of My message. It has kept dry through the season of
construction because of your commitment and sacrifice in
the midst of all the seasons of abandonment.

Now, they too, will se that day after day, I have spoken
in dreams and continue to speak. What an elegant,
beautiful woman I have built. It's a colorful example of
how I can take someone who is willing to return to the
places of pain and make her beautiful.

Now, I will have you join the train. There you will find
those wrapped in down hiding. There are others just like
you on this train who are wrapped in the downy wings

of My healing Spirit. It's just that you were the first to poke your head out. The message that you carry is one of learning how to be informal with your Father; sit on His lap and become trained by Him.

I Ditched You

What happens when you give up way too early?
When it should have been later on?
Others stuck fast while you dropped out?
What about that?
When your hope dried up while theirs seemed to stay?
What happened there?
I made excuses for my behavior and pretended
it wasn't my fault.
I tossed the doubt to the other party like a hot potato
at a party.
I hid behind my seared conscience and
the reasoning of my friends.
It was a fire fed by smoldering resentment for dreams
never met with fulfillment.
Lost hope piled upon lost hope like dirty laundry
in my mind became the next wash load.
Setting my need to move on as pre-imminent,
I ditched you.

You must have been Beautiful

You must have been beautiful in your unfallen form
Oh, the mar of sin, despair of soil,
pain of ire, joy of Satan's spoil.

You must have been beautiful
White robes glistening in the sun
Flowing glory rippling in the breeze with ease
A glide for a stride,

You must have been beautiful.
Fallen morning star, you are where you are.
Inept, unkept, unsure, insecure,
Undone, unsung
A song without a tune, a sun without a moon.
Despaired, despoiled, marred, soiled
Linen in the rain, silk in the dew
Spots of pain running through.

Birth with regret, grown without honor
Blind to see the me in me
Eyes of the world fix my gaze
Caught with each step in a misty haze.

I must have been beautiful, before
That was then.

But, what of now, is there hope for today?
Or has my day of glory passed without my say?
Caught in a net I can't forget
Regret builds regret
Am I inept?

I must have been beautiful
Created for good will
Tucked in the womb; my mother's thrill.
But, what of now, am I still?

Stepping out of our Vehicle

The Dream:
*There is a difference between allowing others to
dismantle your vehicle due to lack of attentiveness and
having your husband come in and drive it off. Sometimes
He has us step out of our vehicle, not to dismantle it, but
put it in the garage for later.*

Interpretation:
God gives purpose and direction with ministry and we
are all gung ho. Yet, sometimes He asks us to step aside
from that primary purpose. We become confused about it.
The dream indicates that, sometimes, he wants to shelter
us for a while so we can be in a place of protection.

The Union

The Dream:
The radio announcer ended up in my bed. I didn't do anything immoral, yet I felt that I was unfaithful in two ways. He was a young, fair man who needs to finish high school He has a year to go. I didn't know him or desire to be with him, but he came on to me and I didn't resist him. I was passive and permitted him to move in on me and he nearly took advantage of me. And, I know that my unfaithfulness isn't to my husband, but to myself and to God.

Interpretation:
This is an announcement that someone is going to try to take advantage of me, but it will be interrupted. He will be caught. I am caught, as well, yet I haven't done anything immoral, even though some may try to say that I have. This week the management at my hospital (as a hospital employee) asked me to be in a movie. They wanted to make me a 'star'. But, I followed the recommendations that God gave in the dream, and I called my 'mission control advisor' and he saw right away that they were attempting to take advantage of me. He was caught in the act of trying to put the move on me in a bad way.

Vehicles of Coercion

The Dream:
I couldn't seem to find my way back to the base medical where I belonged. I ran the periphery and came to many touring people who were being put into these funny cars that they were unable to steer. The vehicles had been all lined up for them to go on this tour, but they were very inappropriate.

Interpretation:
Many are given a vehicle that they are expected to get into, but it is wrong. Others are lining them up to see what they want them to see, not what they have paid for. It's a bad tour in the wrong vehicle. The Union is wrong and the Management is wrong. When they line these things up and expect others to go along with their tour, it is not right. These are vehicles of coercion and violence forcing people to go 'your way' or no way.

Two hearts

I have two hearts. One to be known and one to know Him.

There are two hearts. I love Him and I love them. They know my heart, but He knows a different one. So, am I two different people? No. I am a thread. It's just that I am different colors at each end.

I gave you dreams and pointed some things out. Something old gets added, others need to change. Some feel you should end it all. But, I prove that it is not theirs. I have a right to write, sharing my heart through yours. For, I have a right to be here.

I am working pretty hard to be there on time with everyone else before the class starts. But, I have obstacles. There are many against me. even my own husband is making things hard. He would rather I continue to write, but never move out to publish. I am a nobody. My name doesn't work to get me places. I scoot in just in time to grab the last seat. Even that is facing the wrong direction. I need to turn it around to be able to pay attention to the teacher. There are old places that are surfaces they used to write on; desks. I need to turn over the old lessons God has taught me. Turn them around.

My pen is taken. Others will take up what I am doing because they see it flows for me. They want it. The girl in my dream thinks it is my pen that flows. It is really the Spirit that flows. I don't really need a pen. But, I need the flow. Others pick up on the flow. But, I won't be empty because the flow isn't from me. They think it is. There is a special trend toward salvation and newborns.

I'm the fall guy but I drive down toward the seasons in my vehicle. It's a seasonal fruit truck. I drive through the orchard.

52

Second Hand Love

The Dream:
They had a festival. I am not sure why, but I came to the very end and saw that they were selling things for those named "Sherry". It's not spelled right, but I appreciate the thought. And, what they do is sold by hand.
Why would I buy something that will probably not fit because it is not made for me, merely carries my name misspelled?

Interpretation:
It is a ploy to make money: that they try to look personal, but aren't. No one is fooled. Either someone knows you or he doesn't. It all boils down to relationship.

There are those declaring their own party time. They sell things with My name on it; garments hand made, elegantly stitched, colorful and set on hangers ready for market.

But, it's really a swap meet. What they are looking for is to swap their products for your money. It's a lure to pad their pockets.

I don't buy it, and neither do others. Why would I buy a book, a song, a sermon, or a piece of art just because someone signed My name to it? I prefer to write My own books, sing My own songs, teach myself and paint My own pictures. It is just that they don't know how to open the flow of their spirit to Me and allow My Spirit to flow through their hands onto the paper.

And, do they think others buy it? They don't. When they do their own work, but tack My name to it, others recognize that work isn't from Me. They aren't fooling anybody. It's obvious because the garments that they stitch don't fit Me. They are the wrong size and color.

Suppose your husband drinks coffee with cream and sugar and someone comes along claiming to know him and orders his coffee in the restaurant. Suppose that person orders the coffee black. Wouldn't it be obvious to all around that he doesn't know him when he shows up? Of course.

And, the same is true with God. The only ones that they fool are others who don't know Me either. Then, there are those who make their hearts desire, yet tack My name to it as an after thought in an effort to try to sell it. Are they trying to sell it to Me or trying to sell others on the idea that they know Me? Is it an attempt to be known by God or an attempt to look spiritual? Neither happens.

God is not bribed by anything we do. We cannot do a good work, then ask for His approval. He desires, not our works, but obedience to his voice. It He has told us to learn to love our brother, yet we ignore His words and pursue a career of becoming an evangelist, God may not be pleased. We have ignored His command and launched out our own. We have chosen works of our own convenience attempting to trick God and others that we love Him. God is not tricked and neither are our brothers. For our brother knows that we do not love him.

In our attempt to make money we misspell God's name on the tag of the garment we stitch.

We have heard others say it and know how it sounds. We have seen true ministry based on intimacy with God, so we have an idea of how it should look. But, it didn't originate from our relationship with us to Him. It's second hand intimacy and like soup warmed over, it misses the aspect of being fresh.

I can tell you about me and someone; then I can tell you about someone else's relationship with him. It's not the same. Second hand sales.

And, like going to the thrift store, the can tell if it's

new or used. You can shine it up, dress it up, polish it, and wrap it fancy, but they still know. Why? How do they know?

Because, they will look at your face and into your eyes. Do your eyes dance when you speak of your lover? Does your voice tremble when you describe your times together alone? Is there a pull to the corner of your lips and a sparkle in your eye as you recount the words just as He whispered them into your ear?

If He did, then you do. If He didn't, then you don't.

How do you know two lovers are in love? You know. How do you know the story is first hand? You do. So do others.

You are not fooling anyone by claiming intimacy with God that doesn't exist. There is no such thing as second hand love.

Chapter 4

HISTORY
Who they said I was

A World Turned Upside Down

The Dream:
The rain and the wind come against this house by the sea. My youngest daughter and some others were there. Then, the house rolled over. I wasn't afraid because I saw it before, when it happened to me.

I thought that surely we will drown, but we didn't. Again, we rolled in slow motion to end up in a field. A twister came and I saw it coming. I yelled at my youngest daughter to protect her. She barely got out of the way of destruction. And, I saw it again in the distance. It will certainly return. She just stands there unaware of the danger do close at hand.

Interpretation:
The trial and test to those who see what God has for them is about to come. My daughter is in the midst of a huge turn over. At this point it is surrounded by the environment of their time. The time is at hand when God pours our His Spirit.

The Spirit doesn't move; we move. The entire Church is about to be turned upside down. The line where He will pull us through is tight. It is a hook of love strong but delicate.

So, even in the midst of the storm, He will pull the Church through. As it looked like the Church would die, I knew it wouldn't. I have been here before, myself. Rock and roll, then turn overs.

When He turns your world upside down, do you stay where you are? Are you stabilized by things apart from this world? It is the place resting in His peace.

Infected Wounds

First, we come to Him, then, we carry out the trash. Follow the incision to the infection. It's a wound that causes pain and suffering. The person needs to be opened up. Only, when he opens up, the wound, can God work to bring healing and deliverance. Not all wounds need an incision and drainage. Some just need an exploration with the great Physician. For, the exploration brings him face to face with the truth.

Deliverance is not a breakfast we can cook up for another. Our grill is to egg them on to take the egg off their face in places they cannot see and reach. (This is the outline for Sinactia).

Faking Flute

The Dream:
They handed me a flute and I tried to play it. I had lessons in grade school, but was never very good even then, so this time I just faked that I could play it. Perhaps they noticed. The instructor requested for me to go across campus and do something for her. So, after a complicated journey I located the place and went up the long flight of stairs. I was surprised to see it was a part of the school as well. Students began arriving for class and I realized it was a theatre class. Some looked as though they were still in high school even though it was supposed to be a college class. This is quite interesting and I think I am a better fit for this class than the other. Looks like I am a better fit for stage performance.

Interpretation:
When others put you into their expectations it is a sure recipe for failure.

House of Horrors

The Dream:
I was in line in the red truck. I came to some steps and had a hard time getting up them with out running the person over in front of me. So, I asked him to step aside or move forward. So, I pushed him and continued to wait my turn. At it came, I saw with this ride we all take our chances.

I waited within the vehicle God had given me. He has given me the ability to hear His voice and pray in the answers. When I came to the steps, I wanted to move faster than others. I found those in front of me and those who stalled at certain steps. We have steps at our own rate, but we can push forward if we desire. It is a personal walk and we all take our chances on the steps.

And, we each enter the house of horrors differently. The guy in front of me went on around and the girl climbed on a shelf, but neither of them was going anywhere. I went through the front door. For I figure, I may as well get it over with. It's only a ride and there have been many before me go on this ride and came out the other side.

So, I enter the haunted place and hands reach out to molest and tickle me. I check and they are not human hands; no flesh and blood in those hands. These mechanical hands grab me and pull me back with such force that I know now I must be on a fast track. It's a ride of molestation. I am sure the face will change soon. All just ways to try to scare me from going into this haunted place.

Interpretation:
As I progressed in my walk with God, He led me through the places where my defeats existed in my past. It was a place of my 'horrors'. Within this dream the

place of my past horrors is depicted like a roller coaster in a haunted house. He says that when we reach this step where we must deal with our past, some stall and are put on a shelf. They go no further because they are not willing to face their horrors and take the ride to meet them again where they will receive victory. It is like an infected wound that must be opened up to become healed. If the wound remains closed, it will never become healed. The woman in the dream was shelved because of her reluctance to open areas of hurt in her past.

There is a man in front of me who is standing on the steps that lead toward the 'ride of horror'. He chooses to go around this ride. He avoids the hurts of his past and because of his avoidance, he goes backwards in his walk with God.

But, I figure that I may as well get it over with. Others have faced their past and received healing from God, so I may as well try. What I find is that the hands which molested me as a young girl were not hands of flesh, but of the evil one; the Devil. He was the one who was behind the things which were done to me as a child.

And, the face of the sin changes as I ride the return to the horrors of my childhood. What I find is that the face of the torment changes, but the one behind it remains the same; it is not human, but spiritual torment brought on by a hand of the Devil. And, with this return to the places of my haunted life, they continue to scare me off so that I will not continue to go there. For, the enemy wants to keep me infected with the hidden sin of my past. But, one by one I open those infected areas and allow my Father to bring His healing salve and cleansing.

Changing Litter

The Dream:
The grandparents were away, so I went to the house to check on it. I was astonished that the cats were there. Certainly, they should have been taken care of. So, I changed their litter.

Interpretation:
My forefathers have tripped, but, now I have been sent to check on what they left undone. Changing the litter would be like tending to some cleaning that needs to be done. We need to clean up after our forefather by taking out the trash.

Duel with Sin

Find the devil in your life and meet him there.
Then, kick him out.
Go to the depths of sinfulness and duel with it.

Our Back Room

There is a place in us which we forgot about. It is a place and a time when we were young. Because when we were young, we received so much training, that, now we are older, sometimes we neglect the earlier things we were given.

It's a place when we went from training wheels to learning to balance on our own. Our life was young and we were energetic. So many ideas were birthed into us that we can scarcely count them all. It is a childhood of memories packed with trips to the zoo and birthday parties decorated with streamers and balloons.

But, amidst these memories embedded within our heart are disappointments. Our relatives notice. They know the times we have cried when we failed to receive what our heart longed for because we never told anyone. They know when they abused us with belts, fists, roaming hands and cruel words.

And, these events have also added to our training. As much as we would like to seal that room off, board it over and forget about it all together, we cannot obliterate it from our mind because this room is attached to our house. Like a bedroom we have forgotten about, it is on the other side of our house. And, occasionally, we take out those old places of hurt and feed them. Like animals at the zoo, we release them to the petting area occasionally. We take out our pet peeves and comb over them, reviewing the biggest animals we harbor in this back room of our mind.

But, what of the snake? In a dream, the snake comes to my bedroom and I gather a team to chase it down and eradicate it. The snake symbolizes the Devil as he came to Adam and Eve in the garden. He, too, has lives in this back room because he was there with our training ever since we were children. To think that he desires to train children to hate, be despaired, lonely and lie is the truth.

But, as we grow up, perhaps we caused ourselves some grief with our own sin. Certainly, our family added to bad training, but Satan was there all along attempting to destroy us. His goal is to kill, steal and destroy. He is the one behind those who steal our innocence and promote lying and greed. He is the one who is behind the destruction of family unity.

Our image of the influence of Satan is so tainted that we cannot recognize him when he slithers into our bedroom interrupting our sleep. When we call on the wisdom of God, He will help us to see the difference between good and evil. God's wisdom does not run from the Devil in our dreams, because he is not there. God has not given him any authority within dreams. It is our image of him that enables him to slither into our dreams, not that he is actually there. Our fear of him is what enables him to keep us from pursuing him, just like a snake coming into our bedroom. We are afraid of it, so we run instead of pursuing. If we fear the entrance of the Evil one into our dreams, then we allow him in by way of that fear. He isn't there, but the fear we have of him is. It's our fear of him, not him that we feel.

When we call on the wisdom of God, coupled with the presence of the Holy Spirit, we will be able to spot the areas of fear and clear out misconceptions related to interpreting dreams within our lives for today. We need to enter the areas of fear and weed out all that doesn't come from God.

The time has come for us to clean up the training we have received as a child and allow our Father to become a companion; a husband, to accompany us to clean up misconceptions of dreams. He will help us to review those places of training and understand where we have nurtured bad training. He will come with us to the back room of our thinking.

If we have a snake in our back room, then he will slither out into the rest of the house while we sleep. We must be relentless in our pursuit of old sin of our childhood, forgive those who have injured, and pray for healing of these wounds. Only when our eyes are open to see the plans of the Devil, can we see how he affected our childhood. We must forgive our relatives for their cooperation with the snake and release the spirits that come with them: the animals of pain that we harbor in that back room. By authority in the name of Jesus we can kick out the animals of anger, remorse, bitterness, envy and deception (to name a few).

It is God's truth that takes the head of the snake off. As Satan has had his control over events of the past, now we shine the light of truth onto his activities. When we shine the light of truth onto his activities, he dies. The idea of evil dies and gives birth to elements of truth within our past.

Our Father does not force us to turn over areas of our house to His control. As long as we allow the snake to have free run of our house, he continues. We must ask for God's help to scout out the areas of evil and kick them out, and then patch up the cracks that allowed him to enter in the first place. As we allow our Father to join in going to those places of our past, He will reveal the intentions of the enemy. Then, as we see the intentions of the enemy, we call it to God's attention and He will take out the purposes of the Devil within that situation. He will bring healing to our lives from the time that we were children.

That is a miracle of God. The event that was birthed
from sin cannot be erased, but the effects of it can. Like
a snowball rolling down hill, the ball starts somewhere
in the past. We cannot stop the past, but we can melt
the snowball to today as it continues to roll down hill.
By forgiving those who have injured us as children, we
prevent the pain from re entering our place of peace today.

Encountering enemies

The Dream:
*I have encountered a skunk and a coyote, but they are
more interested in chasing one another, than bugging me.
Then, when a wolf comes after me, I go to my friend's
house. His dog comes out and protects me. The wolf
becomes a puppy up against the German Shepherd.*

Interpretation:
There are times when I will see enemies pass on by.
If they are not coming after me, then let them pass.
Sometimes, they are simply attacking one another.

The second message is that sometimes, the enemy will
be attacking me. I need to Go to the house of my friend,
Jesus and He will provide protection for me. What the
Devil has against me will become like a puppy, when put
up against the fire power of God.

Hidden Entrances of Evil

The Dream:
There is a snake at our house. It's a huge poisonous one. First it comes into the bedroom, then cruises all over the house. I scream and wake Paul. He knows how to battle snakes, so he is not afraid. We begin to search for it room by room. Mother is there and I tease her at one point telling her the snake is coming when he isn't. It is funny and she rolls on the floor between the stone block walls at first, then hops right up and scurries to safety. We start to track him, then a daughter comes around the corner riding her bicycle. She has been playing with him in a room we forgot all about. There are other animals in that room as well. I have wanted to see some of them, but certainly, I don't want to see the snake.

And, there are people at the doors peering in: on lookers. But, I notice a huge crack in the door and am sure that this is how he got into our house. Paul and I are appalled that the young girl is not smart about playing with it in the back room in a place we have forgotten all about. We built this place, so I wonder how we could forget about rooms.

Now that this room is called to my attention, I will clean it up and use it for guests.

Interpretation:
There is a place in our house which we have closed off. It is a room where we forget the things of our youth. Sometimes we separate ourselves from ourselves in a way that causes us to seem partitioned like a house with rooms boarded over. In this dream, I follow a snake to its entrance. The entrance of evil is like a crack under a door; a place when I was innocent of knowing the difference

between good and evil.

Dreams have opened my eyes to see the evil and my relationship with the Spirit as my husband, has enabled me to hunt it down and rid it from the place where it dwelt. My husband in the dream is like God as a husband to the Church. He is the one who tends me as a plant; like a husband. He also tends to the deliverance from evil when it enters.

In the dream, we meet mother (Wisdom). She is not afraid of the evil that roams, yet she knows how to avoid it. Within her words is the ability to avoid the entrance of evil to our house. She stands by the blocks of understanding the deception of the Devil.

The message in the dream is to track down the evil in your life and rid yourself of it. The Holy Spirit and dreams will help. Where he leads me to is an area I have walled off in the past when I was a child. I mixed evil in with good, not realizing the difference. Now that I am older, He wants me to weed out the evil in my past and get it out of my house.

This dream is not only for me, but for others, that is why they look on. By writing the dreams down and printing them in books, this message will be shared. He is pointing out that many have rooms they have walled off and forgotten about which hold things that are dangerous to them now. They are ideas related to the things of the Evil one which could harm their spiritual growth for today. These need to be separated from the ideas which are good and tossed out of the house. Many ideas are hidden in our subversive from when we were children. They may be a hazard to us.

This dream bares a promise that God will show us areas that are entrances of the enemy in our lives. If we see children, then, we need to consider if that child is us.

Once we deal with these areas where the Devil has

had free run, then after he is chased out, this becomes an area where our lives can be used to serve others. If we are hiding an element of sin in an era of our life history, then God can't use it to enable healing for others. The sin must be rooted out and destroyed, for God only uses pure vessels to serve His wine to others.

Drugging Children

The Dream:
One of my daughters, Stephanie Hope, was very distraught because her sister, Joy, was moving out. She had been upset before this time, but those who were her care givers had given her drugs to keep her quiet. In the dream I say, "It is apprehensible to give drugs to a child because you do not want to hear their cries."

Interpretation:
I think the dream tells us a couple of things. Let me interpret it a couple of ways. Number one is by using their names. ....Hope for these children have been without consolation. They have been torn from their families. Their joy has been removed and replaced with that likened to drugs. None wants to hear their cries, so they dull the cries before they are able to reach those who would care.

The natural relationship of what would console these children has been removed and they are distraught. It is as if what they have grown up with (by relationship) is being torn from them. They are traumatized. Yet, others have rendered them useless... as drug addicts... street throw always. The label which has been applied is not applied by the value of the children but by uncaring adults; those who have stripped them of their identity and dulled their sense of who they are. It is apprehensible what has been done to them.

Tricked by the Devil

God doesn't suddenly become father when we ask Him to. He has been our father all along. It's us that have failed to realize it. We are like ducks that when hatched from our shell, followed the first ones we saw. We followed and followed who we thought was our father but he is illegitimate. He has stopped in and placed his stamp on that which is another's. He has staked claim to that which is Gods; us.

Then, he twisted the idea to feed us lies about our true father didn't love us and abandoned us at birth. He told us that it was his good nature to step in where God failed. And he said, "Look in the mirror. Don't you see how much you look like me?"

And we did. We have looked in the mirror of Satan's deception and believed the lies. But, he is a liar. It is God who is our true father. By His hand we have been made. Not only has He provided everything we are made of, He provided the plans. He sees the plans as finished by His provision.

But, because we couldn't see him, we thought He didn't exist. And why couldn't we find Him? Did he abandon us? Did we look for a spirit with our flesh? We cannot find God if we never step beyond our plane. This world is like the womb of a woman. If we stay inside the womb we can never get His world.

We must be released from that womb of the kingdom of

this world into the a new place: the Fathers kingdom. We must be born again.

But, you say, "We are already alive."

So is a baby tucked within the womb. We must be born again a spiritual birth and from a spiritual egg to see who our true father is. Our true father is waiting just outside the womb with a receiving blanket and arms out stretched to cleanse us and wipe the tears from our face and wrap us in His love.

Questioning Clairvoyance

Clairvoyance is contacting the spirit domain. Individuals make it sound amazing and miraculous that they could tap into regions unknown to our flesh. Do they talk to people that are dead? Reason with me...

If someone passed from this earth to be in the presence of God Almighty, to be made perfect, whole and righteous, he walks the streets of gold, singing praises to the Lord, what would encourage him to drop back to the fallen, sinful world, go into the mind of a person he doesn't know, who is charging you for a 'service' and share information with you?

Heaven is a party with Jesus. Once our feet leave this earth, there is no looking back. There is no indication to believe that we can. It has appointed for man to die once, and after that we come face to face with Jesus. We face Him for what we have done with what He has told us to do. Whatever revelation of Jesus, he has given to us, we will be held accountable for. This is the judgment seat of Jesus. It is like going to court. If we have claimed his blood as payment for our sin, we will be given a pass to enter Heaven. If not, then we will be judged for our own sins. I really don't see much time in there for talking to those who are claiming to be clairvoyant.

In a wave of the future, I will come from the past; the bottom to the top and turn the world inside out and upside down. Everything hidden will be exposed; my hidden glory, your hidden sin; my hidden purposes for your benefit and Satan's hidden purposes for his intent. But, you can push Heaven forward, if you like. Ask.

Bend

We live to let go.
We die to bury that which is not eternal.
Only through death of that which is not eternal,
will we pass into that which is eternal.
Put away the temporal and pick up the eternal.
Why cling to the rose which will die when you can
have perpetual fragrance?
Live the life
Exact the change
Extend your hand
Fulfill the plan
Devote your life, end the strife
Words and worry, brief grief
May your stride override the chide
Extend to mend: Bend

Recognizing the Beast

The Dream:
There is abandoned property and we walk through the house and out into the back yard. We came this way because the father wanted to bring his son to show him some things. This property is abandoned and left for many years unattended. Our focus is not on the house but the property and the three of us (the father, myself and his small son) out into the back yard. It opens up into a huge property of many acres.

There are small beasts slaughtered and skewered on the fence posts around the property. Unnerving and somewhat weird, one would wonder why the owner had mounted these small creatures at low levels. And, I worried for the son wondering how it would affect him to see such violence done to these small beasts. But, the father didn't seem to pause as he walked his son by the small beasts who had been killed and now strung up as symbols to ward off intruders. We were surrounded by the small symbols of death on every side. Certainly, a squirrel on a fence post is weird, but not too scary.

Yet, his father wanted to show him the abandoned property, so we went there.

And, as a demonstration of mercy for that which is abandoned we begin to tend to some of the areas that need help. There is a lot of unnecessary structures built on the property. They are fences. Most likely de-fenses. I begin to focus on the one closest to the porch. It blocks the view from the porch to the backyard. It is a chunk of chain-link fence reinforced and held into the ground with cement pillars. It is just structure without purpose; fortification which does nothing except make the property look bad. They are chains with links leading to nowhere. Rough and tough, sturdy and well developed, but useless except to devalue the property by making it look bad. I try to tear the fence down, but it is too big, so I leave it and move onto other areas of the yard.

My friend down a few really tall weeds in the middle of the yard and I wondered if he was going to clean up the entire mess, but he stopped short of it because the mere size of it was so overwhelming.

As we press on to continue our tour of the property, we come to one fence structure after another intended to keep people from crossing over into his property. We went from one structure to the next tearing down de fences.

And, way out in the back area we found a well fortified fence. It guarded against allowing the poor access. It was like a one-way library book drop. They could drop their deposits in, but never had access to them again. Whatever they dropped into the 'boxes' became the 'property of the owner' because it was now on his property. The fence was made of steel covered over by cardboard so that the poor were familiar with it... because many poor live in card board boxes. But, they were like mail boxes in that they had a one way door and the owner came to retrieve what the poor gave (in good conscience) and kept it as his personal property. The fence structure was like a 'Good Will' depository in that the poor felt that if they gave of what they didn't need, then they were doing something good to help provide for other poor people. And, the things that they gave were accepted, but the other side of the equation was never completed because the property is abandoned and the owner has long since died. The poor continue to give to these structures thinking that they are helping other poor people, but the good pile up without their knowledge. The structure intended to assist the poor does not because there is no one to manage it. Remember, the property is abandoned.

74

Then, all of a sudden, out of the corner of my eye I notice the antlers of a huge beast (quite possibly a moose). No doubt he is beside (himself) on this property. There are only a few fences between he and I, so I recognize the threat and make run from the situation. You see, I think that this wild beast lives on the property feeding off of it. We are considered 'intruders' on the property which he has decided that he owns by virtue of his size. I recognize a big beast and have no desire to come face to face with him, so I yell at the father and the son and we begin to backtrack from the property and through the house.

Interpretation:

There is an abandoned property and we walk through the house and out into the back yard. We came this way because the father wanted to bring his son to show him some things. This property is abandoned and left for many years unattended. Our focus is not on the house but the property and the three of us (the father, myself and his small son) out into the back yard. It opens up into a huge property of many acres.

There is abandoned property which the Father wants to bring us onto. He wants to show some things to His children. He wants teach a lesson. This is a lesson on abandoned property, the poor and the guarding of it all by the beasts. This area is huge. For the purposes of this dream the focus is not on the individual (house) but what is left for him/her to take care of because of the Father showing it to him/her. It is about caring for those things that have been left in our keeping by another. They were important to those who have gone on before. I believe there are anointing and jobs which were given to those who have passed on before that still need to be done, yet we have neglected them like abandoned property. We have failed to do maintenance on these areas, so they are not being useful to others.

There are small beasts slaughtered and skewered on the fence posts around the property. Unnerving and somewhat weird, one would wonder why the owner had mounted these small creatures at low levels. And, I worried for the son wondering how it would affect him to see such violence done to these small beasts. But, the father didn't seem to pause as he walked his son by the small beasts who had been killed and now strung up as symbols to ward off intruders. We were surrounded by the small symbols of death on every side. Certainly, a squirrel on a fence post is weird, but not too scary. Yet, his father wanted to show him the abandoned property, so we went there.

When we first go to this place we are greeted by unsettling 'guard posts'. We don't give them much attention because of their size. The demonic world has posted guards to help keep out 'intruders' that would come to tend the fields that are abandoned. These are 'small things' that scare people causing them to feel uneasy about the situation. For instance someone gives you a car to pass on to someone else, but not all of the paperwork is completed for its release. This could make you begin to question the transaction and 'scare you off' from doing it. The fields of abandonment are those areas of ministry which have been abandoned. They are places of 'ownership' that individuals have failed to take up residency. There are many 'jobs' that God would like to give, yet He does not have anyone to do them…and the dream gives insight into several reasons why these properties continue to be abandoned.

And, as a demonstration of mercy for that which is abandoned we begin to tend to some of the areas that need help. There is a lot of unnecessary structures built on the property. They are fences. Most likely de-fenses. I begin to focus on the one closest to the porch. It blocks the view from the porch to the backyard. It is a chunk of chain-link fence reinforced and held into the ground with cement pillars. It is just structure without purpose; fortification which does nothing except make the property look bad. They are chains with links leading to nowhere. Rough and tough, sturdy and well developed, but useless except to devalue the property by making it look bad. I try to tear the fence down, but it is too big, so I leave it and move onto other areas of the yard.

Mercy is the gift where you give to another's need without return. The other has no ability to return anything and is totally in need. The property is a perfect example of a demonstration of the gift of mercy because the owner is dead and the property is abandoned. It cannot do anything for itself and needs someone else to manage it. In the dream there is no indication that, by cleaning up the property, any of us who are visiting the property will obtain it; we just see a need and try to help. There is nothing for us to gain except sweat, sore muscles and time spent working on someone else's property. Even the owner isn't there to appreciate it because he is dead. Giving within the gift of mercy has no personal benefit. It is 'giving' in the most holy form.

What I see are that 'within the field of giving and receiving property' there are several structures. Indeed, when we 'give' to Church and 'give' to individuals, there is a great difference. Some things are set in stone, while others are not. I think this part of the dream refers to our teaching. We have been taught a specific way regarding how and who we should give to. We have been provided with 'ready made' defences which rise up against situations. This compares to the sturdy fence which I attempted to get rid of in the back of the house, but couldn't because it had been overbuilt. Giving to non-profit organizations which have overbuilt structures is one example of how this 'de-defence' does no real good, but only gets in the way. The structure of organizations is often very costly and takes a lot away from those for whom the intended organization is originally set up for. What the dream says is that, try as we may, these structures are here to stay and their defence is too strong to tear up. Many Churches give a set percentage of their 'Mission' income to 'set charities'. They give to uphold the structure without regard for the purpose. That is an example of a fortified defence to 'give' to a structure which does no purpose because of the way or the place in which it is set up.

My friend whacks down a few really tall weeds in the middle of the yard and I wondered if he was going to clean up the entire mess, but he stopped short of it because the mere size of it was so overwhelming.

In this part of the dream, my friend takes a sickle and begins to chop down weeds. Weeds are symbolic of those things that have grown up in place of that which is supposed to grow there. There are specific areas of ministry which God intends for true ministers to be grown...but because of the abandonment, weeds have taken over. The homeless shelters which have 'sprung' up fill in the gap in the places where that which was supposed to be no longer exists. People continue to have needs and if the Kingdom of God does not meet those needs, then they will look for other ways to meet their needs. We cannot think that we will be able to take out these other agencies on our own. We may be able to take out a few of the really bad ones, but certainly we cannot handle the task of tackling the entire field. Remember, we don't own the field, but are given an opportunity to demonstrate mercy within it. There is no ownership within the Kingdom of God. We are all stewards to the King.

As we press on to continue our tour of the property, we come to one fence structure after another intended to keep people from crossing over into the property. We went from one structure to the next tearing down de fences.

The dream is a window to understanding the ways of the Kingdom of Darkness operating against those who desire to enter into the fields of abandonment. Remember that our goal is to demonstrate mercy on the property that is abandoned. We remove that which has been put into place (by the Kingdom of Darkness). They are structures without business; walls without purpose. They are defences which the enemy puts up to keep others away from entering into this place. He has built structures, like fences without gates that are given 'in defence' of protecting the property. The purpose is to protect the property from those who could actually benefit from it, no to keep out illegitimate users. The end of the dream reveals that the 'beast' has claimed this abandoned property and intends to keep it.

There is similarity between the small scary beasts and the fences in that they are both meant to scare off would-be users, or those who would show mercy within this vacancy. The fences are akin to the word defences. What the message is that the Kingdom of Darkness has built many defence mechanisms with the intention of keeping the Children of God from moving across into the land of opportunity; into those areas of vacancy. This property was meant to show mercy to the poor and the Kingdom of Darkness has built a fortress of defence to keep others from crossing. In the dream we begin tearing down these structures one by one.

And, way out in the back area we found a very well fortified fence against allowing the poor access. It was like a one-way library book drop. They could drop their deposits in, but never had access to them again. Whatever they dropped into the 'boxes' became the 'property of the owner' because it was now on his property. The fence was made of steel covered over by cardboard so that the poor were familiar with it...because many poor live in card board boxes. But, they were like mail boxes in that they had a one way door and the owner came to retrieve what the poor gave (in good conscience) and kept it as his personal property. The fence structure was like a 'Good Will' depository in that the poor felt that if they gave of what they didn't need, then they were doing something good to help provide for other poor people. And, the things that they gave were accepted, but the other side of the equation was never completed because the property is abandoned and the owner has long since died. The poor continue to give to these structures thinking that they are helping other poor people, but the good pile up without their knowledge. The structure intended to assist the poor does not because there is no one to manage it. Remember, the property is abandoned.

The interesting thing about the dream is that the whole property is abandoned while this one corner in the back is full of activity on the other side of the property line. The poor continue to give without realizing that there is no way for what they are giving to be given to anyone else. This dream reveals a secret tactic of the Kingdom of Darkness to those who give. They give with the expectation that what they have to offer is going somewhere, but it isn't because the other side of the depository is not open. It is a line of givers without any receivers. People line up to give, but none receive back because there is no one to do the work of returning what they have given. There is no one to process what they have given and turn it around because the place is abandoned.

In the dream the poor people don't realize that they are giving to a dead system. The good will of men goes nowhere. Men may will for good to be done to others, but it is only by the mercy of God that true good will happens.

Then, all of a sudden, out of the corner of my eye I notice the antlers of a huge beast (quite possibly a moose). No doubt he is beside (himself) on this property. There are only a few fences between he and I, so I recognize the threat and make run from the situation. I thought we might find this neighbor here. You see, I think that this wild beast lives on the property feeding off of it. We are considered 'intruders' on the property which he has decided that he owns by virtue of his size. I recognize a big beast and have no desire to come face to face with him, so I yell at the father and the son and we begin to backtrack from the property and through the house.

The central message of the dream is that I have spied the Beast on the abandoned property and none of the fences between him and me are enough to keep him from coming at me to cause terror and destruction. An elk or Moose is the largest of the deer family and tramples to kill. One of the interesting things I found in the dictionary was that the 'Moose' organization in the US has one of their philanthropic programs which provides for abandoned children.

God's Enemy or Ours?

There is an erroneous idea being propagated that Satan is God's enemy. How silly is that?

If Satan was Lucifer, a fallen angel from heaven, then, certainly he knows about the power of the most high God. And, if Lucifer raised himself up to be like God so that others would bow down before him, then, he knows enough about the power of God to desire to mimic it. He realizes that the power of God is great. And, if, when he raised himself up against God when in heaven, and was tossed out of heaven by Michael and a few other angels, then, certainly, he realizes that, he is still out numbered and out powered 2 to 1. For, I believe, he can count, and if I remember the story, one third of the angels were thrown from heaven with him when they joined forces with him to raise themselves up to be like God. If you look at that battle described in Revelation, it never mentions God joining in the fight. Lucifer was thrown out of heaven by the word of God and the hands of the angels who remained loyal to God.

So, Satan doesn't fight God. He has already lost that battle. Why would he raise up against an enemy when he is certain to meet defeat every time? Remember, God created him. How much greater is the creator than the created being? Could the created thing ever think to raise up against that which created it? Does the pot talk to the potter, or the painting to the artist?

No, Satan raises himself up against us. The Children of God and the other angels who remain faithful to the purposes of God are his enemies. When he comes against us with spiritual vision for his evil purposes, and we do not look with our spiritual eyes, then we don't see him coming. He becomes like a semi-truck who would side swipe a sedan. We see him in the rear view mirror barreling down upon us, yet we are powerless to escape from impending wreckage.

Think about it: If the enemy destroys the descendents, then there will be no one to carry on the family name and uphold the banner. If he takes out the kids, then he will destroy the race. He desires to win the race, and defeat his enemy in any way possible. He can't win the war, but he certainly, can inflict severe casualties on the other side. And, when the soldiers have tremendous casualties, they, often spend so much time patching up the troops that they have no time to arm themselves against their enemies. As he inflicts wounds in our brothers and sisters, mothers and children, then we focus on them and forget to watch our own flank. We become sidetracked with worrying about our daughter on drugs or our mother caught in a cycle of depression that we skip Church and make light our prayers to move on to 'doing' something about the predicament. We may focus on activities to bring healing to our loved one, rather than the healer, himself.

Satan has changed our focus from seeking God and hiding behind His protection for us, to raising an occasional shield in defense only when we see arrows flying in our direction. What we find, is that, while we are focused on our crumbling families, he lays a trap of barbed wire for us to fall into. Before we know it, we are sick, and in need of care for ourselves. We, too, have become a war casualty.

And, we thought Satan was God's enemy, so He should fight him. We seek the good things from God, and leave the fighting to Him. This is not true. For, when we neglect to fight the enemy, he will sneak in and overrun our camp, stealing our supplies and pouring out our water.

We must be on the lookout for the enemy and take time with every prayer session to ask God to reveal his position and push him 'way back' from our lives and the lives of our children. It's easy for God. He does it with a breath. Remember? That's how He tossed Satan out of heaven.

Chapter 5

PLANS OF GOD
Who I really am

The Conversation Between Us

It's not about hearing the voice of God as much as it is hearing the conversation between your spirit and His. Then, there are the interjections of your soul, because, of course, your soul doesn't always agree with your spirit. You may not want to reach out to God as your spirit is starving for Him, yet you are pulled by your own beliefs of who He is. Perhaps, they prevent you from seeking Him in a manner that He may be found.

And, what about that conversation: When you hear it and what do you do? I copy it down onto paper, most often.

Come to my spirit, dear Lamb of God. Descend upon this humble heart of mine and lift me to a place that I can only go because of who You are. Oh, precious Father, I pray you would wrap your arms of warmth around me in such a way that I understand Your will. On, send me grace, a spirit of discernment and a continued humble hear that is willing to do Your desire. Spirit of Truth, speak Your message of truth through my lips, I pray. Become in me Your desire. Amen

Victory spirit

The Dream:
And I found my daughter already walking her dog. Like walking into a mirror, I see myself new as I go. But, she needed some spirit so she ordered it and when it was delivered, she couldn't authorize its delivery because she wasn't of age. So, I came to present myself giving authorization for the delivery. And, when I did, the lady held up an old photo of me and compared it to my face now. She seriously questioned if it was the same person because of all of the changes that had been done to my face. Mainly, I noticed that the tooth which once had been twisted and chipped, now is perfect making my smile very beautiful.

The Interpretation:
I'm already walking what I have been given. I already have quite a nice leash on the publishing company. It is compared to walking a dog in this dream in that it needs controlling and cleaning up after. You have to feed and groom it just like a pet.

But, the dream says that I needed something else and put in an order for it. I needed a new spirit. I believe that the spirit of victory is the one that I need. One to know that I have changed and become what I am supposed to be. Victory has been delivered and is knocking at my door, but I need to go and pick it up myself. I need to grab hold of that victory. I surely have changed into someone beautiful.

So, Father, I would like to pick up my new spirit today.
Help me to see as others see me, not as I have always seen
myself; New, different, changed, made into someone mar-
vellous. I would like to pick up my new spirit today
Indeed there is a delivery knocking at my door
Someone has ordered and it is time
The due date has come
Its time to receive
The spirit of victory
And, just how did I get here?

Pushed by a Hand

Pushed by a hand, I cannot feel.
Molded by fingers, I do not see.
Held within his grasp, I live.
Waiting to see what He will make of my life.

Mercy Comes Ashore

Mercy calls again, O Lord, and how do I respond?
Weeping, crying and pounding my chest
Overwhelmed that You have brought me to the rest.
That is how I respond.

Mercy called and I picked up the line
Grace received; I had been deceived, now I know I will be fine
Mercy called, Oh glorious day is at hand
The plans of God will come about as planned.

Mercy has prevailed when pain was all around
Praise His Holy Name. Let His grace abound.

Because this is it. We have reached the end
The mercy boat has arrived.
Truth is here. I do believe it survived
The journey across broken waters, perils, deep and wide
Truth is here, Praise the Lord. Let me confide.
It was long and it was hard. Each day I was on guard
protecting the broad from the shard.
Evil conniving and trickery came to me
Attempting to swoon and make me see
his way instead of God's points of reference
intending to drive me to a place of indifference.

But it didn't work, I refused to go awry
Contending daily, instead, and looking to the sky
To the One and only, the Star that shines eternal
Asking for leading, seeking Wisdom found maternal.
Plotting the course and taking the wheel
going through rough waters, seeking a bigger keel.

An ocean of such great size, given to consume
Something to be respected. I never did presume
Others would help when I tangled in the kelp
Because they didn't.
Again and again I cried out to Him when I went aground,
amiss, awry
And again and again,

He cried back from the hole He had made in the sky.

Mercy calls and how do you respond?
Do you give up and walk to shore, or step through another door?
The desert island called my name as the ship
ran onto the rocks one day.
But, like Noah, I stayed in the boat, got on my knees
intending to pray
And pray and stay on my face unwilling to end the race
until I came to the place where I saw His face. The end of the race.

I believed the promises that put my boat into the sea at start
I believed the mission was true: God wanted to share His heart.
And, like Columbus, perhaps I had no idea where I was going
Was not His intention, but a showing
That I was willing to get into the boat and set it afloat.
I wrote.

Writing after writing; at least that is what I called that stuff.
Because I didn't know what I had. It was like bread in my hand;
all fluff.
Falling from heaven, it came day after day
I waited to see what He had to say.

And the vessel departed the shore and floated on out to sea.
He gave me words and I brought them back to Thee
And, I floated about under the wind of His words,
with prayer as my rudder.
Content to drift, listening, worried that I might stutter
where He didn't.
The question indeed, as I seed
was; Just what did I have?
Not where was I going, or who was I showing,
but staying with the wind to keep the Spirit flowing.
Because the wind pushes the boat, keeps the sails
all billowed up and full.
It's with wind across the starboard, the aft, the bow and the stern
that enables the ship to move, and me to learn
what I need to know to listen and copy the words within their intent
refusing to comply, and insert my lent.
More prayer provides a bigger keel, He kept on saying

So, day after day, night after night, I kept on praying.

And, all the while I drifted further to sea.
The shore in the distance, I had been set free.
To go to the place of His desire, setting my spirit free to fly
into the wings of His anointing as I was calling out to the sky.

And, mercy calls your name, how to you respond?
Tears, cheers and many years, held at sea I have held on.
Keeping the course to the stars, watching for the Son
Listening for every wave, seeing the fish run.
Through currents and storms and waters of unknown depth
This vessel has sailed. All the while I was kept
In His shadow, tucked under His mighty arm
held between the fingertips of God in no alarm.
Like a ring on the finger of a newly married bride
He passed me from one finger to the next; I continued to abide.
Close to the heart and within the grasp He held.
And, do you think He would loose me? Would that ring be felled?
Precious in His sight, covenant of glory,
my open heart to His reveals the story.
Mercy call my name. Beckon me from afar.
Holy Spirit speak to me. Show me who You are.
Bring me to Your house across the might seas
Show me the way, become the say, blow within, bring the breeze

Mercy take flight, blow Your might, become the truth alive
Feed the plan, span the span, grow what You contrived

Mercy play your song, lift the tune. Instruments of delight
God above, precious Dove, may we enter into Your light.
Light of the mercy, light of day, light of night, come have your say.
Dream of God, yet un-met, bring the boat, set the set
vessel of love, voice of the night, blow gentle breeze
to the contrite.
Across their bow. Blessings of adoration. Bring the how.
Show them the way into your port of safe haven for sure.
Direct them, My Lord, show them how to become pure.
Set apart, given a new heart, bring them to You this day.
Across the span to the plan, the place You hear them pray.

Open ears of understanding,
softened hearts ready to praise Your name
Leaving their sin behind them,
content to be released from the blame.
Bring them home, dear Lord I pray
As you have brought me this day.

See the reality with this vessel of knowing Your delight in Me
is that I will pray for others and they will see
You love them as well, but You want to tell
Them Yourself.
So, I will dock my boat and come on ashore this very day
I have reached the destination. I have come to the beach to play.
Sing and dance and collect sea shells. Collect eternal tells.
Voices, echoes and copies of that which is alive.
So, please let me go, I have a vacation to contrive.
Oh, Spirit divine, God from above, I praise Your holy Name,
Enter into Your love.
As I move out of the way and make a way for others.
Open the channels. Become their lover.
Friend, father, sister, brother,
Oh heavenly Father become their mother.
One they can trust to love them at all times
And one who will fill their head and heart with holy rhymes.

And, I thank you for the trip, sometimes it was rough
I have a tendency to get sea sick, I think I have had enough.
Rocking and rolling and skimming across the sea
I am ready for a rest. Thanks for bringing me to Thee.

Contrite Adoration

Contrite adoration comes to my lips as I praise Your Holy name.
My heart is bowed low as I realize I am to blame.
The reason Your kingdom is not expanded and your Name lifted up.
I am to blame for clinging to my cup.

Contrite adoration now comes to my lips.
Within my chest, my heart grips.
Torn apart, broken in two, like communion in Church,
Repentance has moved right through.
For, how can pure love flow from a cup that refuses to be clean?
I have closed my soiled heart, not wanting to be seen.
And, Your water could not flow from this cup because I never went to sup.
I didn't go to Your table, but stayed away instead.
I held to my own views, refusing to be fed.
And, my cup never got washed when I wouldn't bring it to the river.
I refused to seek His mercy and grace. I thought I was the giver.
So, I gave to others all I had. I poured myself out, not realizing it was bad.
Because, the cup was not washed, so the water was tainted.
And, my views weren't cleansed, simply over painted.
With white washed ideas of who I thought God wanted me to be, I showed what was in my hand to others: what I wanted them to see.
But, how could I show them Him when there was so much me within?

Filled with myself, He never came through.
And, this is what I needed to share with you.
For, when I learned to wash the cup, then, that it to His sup
I saw a change in me. I was set free.
And, the He,
He needed to be became free to flow from me to thee.

Benefits of the Blood

It is all about the blood.

Jesus needs dialysis. Does He need purification? Certainly not.

Why would He need dialysis, then?

Because He needs to give purification to others. Only when they connect to Him, can He give the benefits of the blood to them.

The floating body of Christ needs dialysis. They need to go to see and become purified by the washing of the word.

And, the Father is bleeding, as well. And, do we presume to think that we need to draw off of Him when He is already bleeding? His hands are dripping with blood. Why would we not use what He has already given?

It is time to share.

Spiritual Reproduction Clinic

The dream:
I get tired of the family picture portrayed fake. Like
people on stage, we pose for the picture, and then go
back to doing what we want. It's all set and we each are
expected to do our part to make the whole look good.
The whole set up to shoot things causes me nausea, so I
leave and go to the mall. I run into Dr. Martin, the heart
surgeon. He is doing a dance with many others and I join
in. He shows me attention and we end up kissing. And,
instead of asking me to have sex with him, he invites me to
go to a clinic and become impregnated.
I say, "Too weird for me."
Obviously this guy has an extreme desire to have
children and can't take any chances. Somehow I know he
has done it with others. Coming together for the purpose
of having Children is the best part of becoming pregnant.
But he's saying to skip this part because he doesn't want
to take any chances.
I leave never realizing that my skirt is above my waist.
I pass by one who thinks it looks good to be exposed this
way. Still, I say it is not proper, so I cover up.

Interpretation:
Once again we were set to sing. It's a song of intimacy
for the purpose of birthing the expectations of God. Twice
he has met me and loves the dance of the Spirit with his,
but when it comes to Spiritual reproduction, he wants to
take us to a clinical setting. He removes the spontaneity
and sucks the passion from the relationship because he is
not sure about the outcome. He knows the purpose but he
uses the clinical approach at that time because he is afraid

he won't do things right. He doesn't trust that He and Me will be OK without others showing how to put it all together.

Now, tell me: we have two heart surgeons, do you suppose they know how to deal with issues concerning the heart?

Yes, he knows how to operate on the heart, but he is unsure how to operate in. He hasn't learned to trust his heart's ability to be intimate with God.

Death Lie

Of course, remorse is out of the question.
To die is a lie.
Come learn a lesson.
Death is but a sleep
The life He gives is yours to keep.
You can't borrow eternal life.

My New Me

I wish I was what I could be
Alone adrift and totally free
I wish I wasn't what I became
Lost, forlorn, packed with shame
I wish I went to another place
Filled with love; full embrace

I was, I went, I'm done
Full spent. I went full run

What I wish I could, never crossed my mind
The me I found, I never sought to find
How did I get here? Who am I today?
Magnificent peacock tail grace display
Full spread I strut my stuff
Flap my wings and fluff my fluff

I was lent, I did, I'm done
Full spent I went full run

Where I wish I went, was never my desire
This is pure Holy Ghost fire
Aflame ablaze burning love at the heart
I gave mine away at the start
Like a boomerang it returned back to me
For free
You see
He made me free to be my new me

The Response: Spent Kisses

Alone amidst a sea of faces
I looked and none looked back
So, I looked beyond and into their hearts
Shooting love darts
Departs
From anything anyone ever did
I did

You see
Alone amidst that sea of ye
I found the you I came to know
Seeing beyond your face
Through a bubbling sea of grace
Heart to heart seeing eye to eye
I let my restraint go bye, bye

Each kiss I sent was spent and done
Consumed by you on the run
Then, looking for more, you came back
In fact
Continued to stay that way

So, what was I to do with you?
But continue to shower, empower, and devour
Cover with grace, warm embrace
Provide what you need to feed
Your desire for more

Thanks

Holy Spirit Knocks

What does it mean to be filled with the Holy Spirit?
You allow yourself to be encroached on by God's Spirit;
That aspect of him that cannot be touched or seen.
He comes up to you and knocks on the door of your heart.
He has been there lots of times before,
only, this time you open the door.

Birthday Honor

In honor of a birthday of one who was set free.
I give you my heart. I give it to thee.
Early in the morning, late at night
In the mid day until twilight.
I give you myself, I give you my life
I give you my all, come be my wife.
To have and to hold, to keep until the end.
Tucked in my heart, an open end
Like an envelope my soul is open to you
I have tucked you inside, let it be true.
In honor of your birthday, I hold out my hand
Ask you for yours and come to make a stand.
Standing ever true, amidst the promise I made to you.
To have and to keep on until and through
There are no more birthdays, and this era is done
We come to the pause and become one
Then our birthday will meet, yours and mine
We will unite and it will be fine,
A wonderful celebration of love and fun for all
On that glorious day in that heavenly ball.
Happy birthday child, be glad this day
For one who was bound has been freed to say
Happy birthday to others, and happy wedding day
For the celebration is complete and that's all I have to say.
Love Sheri
December 14, 2005
Glory Bound Books Ltd.

CHALISHA INDEX

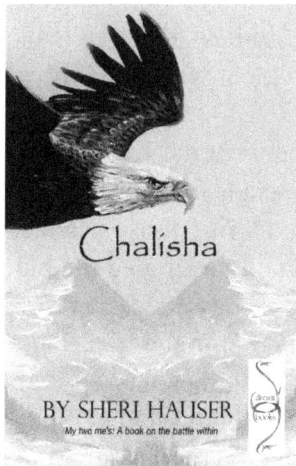

Chalisha

BY SHERI HAUSER

My two me's: A book on the battle within

About the Author

Sheri Hauser is originally from Seattle Washington being raised in a family with three siblings. Both of her brothers have attended seminary and her sister, Karna Peck is a professional artist joining her with many of her books.

At the age of 16 she committed her life to Jesus Christ and began to follow Him wholeheartedly. When she graduated from High School she attended Ecola Hall for extended training in Biblical Studies. Years of Bible Study and memorization are evident within the threads of teaching in her books.

In her early 20's, she went to Nursing School continuing in the field to become a Cardiothoracic Intensive Care Nurse in Las Vegas. During those years, she wrote many of her dream books and developed the publishing company sinking her entire pay check into printing equipment, software tutorials and computers.

Sheri is summed up with these words, "She doesn't just love God. She is IN love with God." She is fanatical about her relationship with God and hearing the voice of God through the power of the Holy Spirit. She has been an active part of many miracles (which you can read about in her books). Her life is like a spiritual light show. Watching the Publishing Company grow from a few books until 2016 is a miracle in itself. She went $140,000 in debt which was settled for $20,000. It took 10 years, but now she has knowledge, experience and equipment; she is glory bound! She retired from the Intensive Care in 2014, and continues to work part time in Home Health Nursing in order to focus more wholeheartedly on the publishing company.

In 2001, she began having dreams with understanding on interpretation of them. The dreams led her to self-publish her first book, Coríanta, and then eventually grow Glorybound Publishing. At the release of this review (2016) she has 23 published books on dreams, from dreams and hearing the voice of God as well as several children's books. In the midst of her training to learn the publishing industry, she also developed the Glorybound Lasertrain which is a set of templates for digital publishing. This set includes 20 books with two text books.

Dream Books

Abreas Ansus English*
Abreas Ansus Spanish*
Abreas Vision Journal
Adoration and Reverence *
Chalisha
Coríanta
Coríanta Love Notes I, II, III
Camezia Reptidad
Dove Dreams Fly
Dreamatrix Immanuel
Festevía
Firefly
Flowing Down River *
Glorybound Publishing Our Way
Glorybound Publishing-Forms
Holy Hum
Kapaseus
Katísha
Manual of Personal Prophetic Prayer
Manual of Church Prophetic Prayer *
Me Mesa
Miracle's
Palagra
Palazzo Lascett
Pillow Talk
Prophetic Interp Art
Reflections of Praise *
Religion *
Seedlings
Sinactia Empezía
Tomaseña
Seed Packet
Wedding Service

Not Completed 12-2016

12 Stepping Stones to the Garden

Ten books which are a series of growing in intimacy with God. These books are written from dreams. The dreams were given over a period of around 6 months or so. As they were received, I carefully interpreted them using Scriptures. Then I was given an outline dream. The dreams of the specific subject were then put into the outline. That forms the DREAM BOOKS. There are more than 12 DREAM BOOKS but these are the 12 which make up the Steps in the Garden. Initially all of the books were as one giant book. Then as I received more dreams of direction the books began to split; first into four, then into 12 (like bread raising in a bowl) they grew over time within the right environment. The first main book was Miracule's. It split into what became the first four books: Miracule's, Katísha, Tomaseña and Coríanta. I was instructed to turn over the stack and release them. So, I released Coríanta having it professionally edited and printed at a cost of $37,000. By the time I got to Tomaseña, I realized that the books were reproducing at an alarming rate and I would never have enough money to print them conventionally, so I asked God if I could have a publishing company.

He said, "Sure."

I quickly responded, "I don't know anything about a publishing company."

His response, "That's OK. It will come in a box with instructions."

I quickly called the guy who put together my first book and then ordered the computer program which he specified as the one for making books. Guess what? It came in a box with instructions. (Smile)

I embarked to study every aspect of publishing and

learned over 12 software options over a period of around 4 years all the time writing my own books. I released Tomaseña and katísha, but when I came to Miracule's I gave it to God as a first-fruit offering because it had been my first book written. Like a first-born child I donated it back to God.

To my surprise, He kept it and said, "Thank You."

Then, He gave me another series of dreams instructing me on how to split Miracule's like a piece of paper on the cutting edge. After about 9 months of extensive study (If you read the book you will see why it took so long) the book was split to become two books; Miracule's and Pillow Talk.

Then I went on to release the rest of the books which are on growing in the gifts and calling of the Holy Spirit.

Coríanta, Tomaseña, Katísha, Miraculeś, Pillow Talk, Camezia Reptídad, Sinactía Empezía, Festevía, Kapaseus, Firefly, Seedlings, Wedding Service.

	**Abreas Ansus** Short book with a dream, a vision and a poem. Spanish and English versions. Hand painted tiles from the gallery of Karna Peck		**Coríanta** It is a collection of shaped poetry, inspirational writings and dreams with interpretative lessons correlated with Scriptures. It is like a box of chocolates; each piece reveals a different flavour of the sweetness of God's heart.
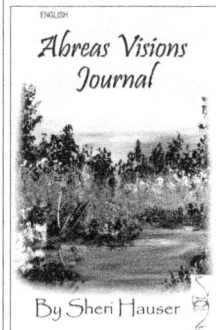	**Abreas Vision Journal** Provides empty paper to write down visions. Included with a short teaching on visions. Has reference to several holy books.		**Corianta Love Notes I-X** A small short book of small words of wisdom which goes along wth Corianta.
	**Camezia Reptidad** The Holy Spirit living within the beliver is compared to seltzer water and we are the ones who add the color and serve to those who are thirsty. We become poured out as a drink offering to others when we serve them with the Holy Spirit as our base adding spiritual gifts.		**Dove Dreams Fly** This is the inside story of how Sheri followed the dreams to hatch a publishing corporation.
	**Chalisha** The internal collision of my two mes. Dealing with mental conflict coming out a winner.	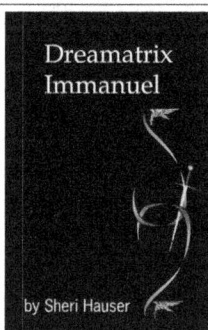	**Dreamatrix Immanuel** A simple manual on interpreting dreams according to Scriptures. It gives dreams, shows errors in interpretation and how to avoid common misconceptions.

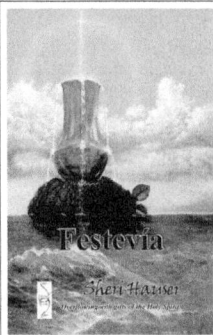

Festevía
We are to share the gifts of the Holy Spirit withint the congregation. We are filled with the light (insight and knowledge) of the power of God and each reflect the light of God with a different color.

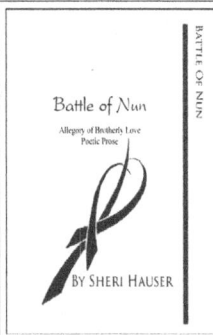

7-Healing Prayers Booklets Seven booklets meant to be read at the hospital bedside. The set comes with blessed healing oil.

Firefly
Dreams are not meant to be 'silent movies'; they have words. The Holy Spirit (Fire of God) flies at night, just like fire flies in the East light up against the dark sky. Learn to get the words message from dreams.

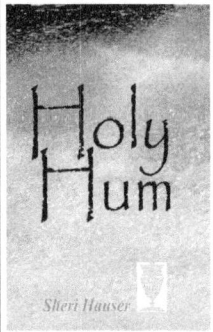

Holy Hum
Shaped Poetry on the subject of the hum of the power of God in the universe.

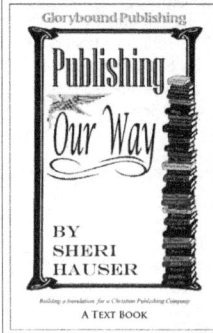

Glorybound Publishing Our Way
Linking with Glorybound Publishing in an international publishing company of your own to publish books. For wanna be Christian publishers.

Kapaseus
It is about leaning on His promises which will bring us through by our faith to achieve His miracles. The book is filled with threads of mercy and strings of hope.

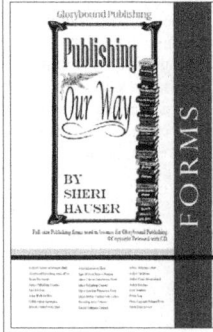

Glorybound Publishing Our Way Forms
Forms which are needed to start publishing company of your own. Includes blank forms and CD.

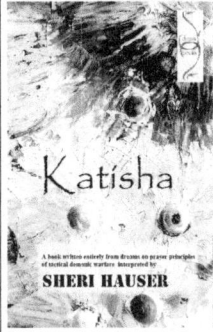

Katísha
A book on tactical spiritual warfare. It compares spiritual Kingdoms and shows how they are at battle and we live in the midst of the war. When we are passive our enemies claim victory.

	**Reflections of Praise** Poetry related to the flow of the Holy Spirit.
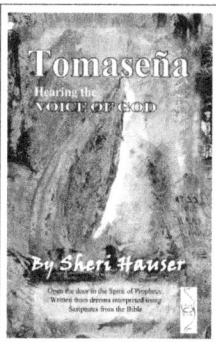	**Tomaseña** A book on the spirit of prophecy, which is hearing the voice of God, from the Old Testament, New Testament in the Bible and today showing that God is speaking the same.
	**Religion** Dealing with Religious spirits.
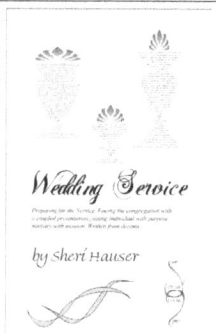	**Wedding Service** The marriage of our vision with the plan; uniting the purpose with the provision moving into ministry.
	**Seedlings** It is about releasing the seeds of ministry to fly simply trusting in Him. And, are we willing to buy seed for others? This book cuts to the heart of service and shows the difference between the true servants of God's Kingdom and those who are the 'hired hands'.
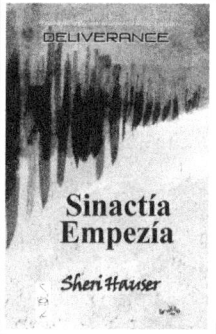	**Sinactía Empezia** A book about deliverance from sin and the consequences of it. The book helps to work through a process of taking spiritual sissors and clipping ties to painful memories of our past.

	Manual of Personal Prophetic Prayer Stepping into Prophetic Prayer for yourself. Powerful use of the gift of tongues, dreams and visions.		**Palagra** Words are black and white on paper like truth is black and white. Teaches responsibility in Christian Writing.
	Manual of Church Prophetic Prayer Working together in a group setting using the gift of tongues, dreams and visions for prophetic prayer.		**Palazzo Lascett** Demonic warfare book about enties (ghosts) in persons, places or things. A look at angelic experiences.
	Me Mesa Shaped Poetry on the subject of anointing.		**Pillow Talk** Spending long nights with Jesus dreaming the right dreams.
	Miracules When we learn to hear His voice, He will not only tell us who He is (apart from all religious injections) but who we are created in Him. The book makes reference to religious books, but is meant not to lead the reader to a specific faith, but to demonstrate God talks to everyone who is willing to listen.		**Prophetic Interpretation of Art** Art has hidden messages and they can be interpreted using the same principles as dream interpretation

dream

books

Made in the USA
Middletown, DE
14 August 2019